Favourite Classic Poets

By Brian Moses

an imprint of Hodder Children's Books

Other titles in the series:

Favourite Classic Writers

Favourite Poets

Favourite Writers

Text © Brian Moses 2003

Editor: Sarah Doughty
Designer: Tessa Barwick

Published in Great Britain in 2003 by Hodder Wayland,
an imprint of Hodder Children's Books.

A Cataloguing record for this book is available from the British Library.

ISBN 0 7502 4291 4

Printed by Wing King Tong, China

Hodder Children's Books
A division of Hodder Headline Limited
338 Euston Road, London NW1 3BH

Contents

William Blake (1757–1827)

To see a world in a grain of sand
And a heaven in a wild flower,
Hold infinity in the palm of your hand
and Eternity in an hour.

William Blake was born in London. As a child he loved poetry and art. From early childhood he claimed to have visions and at the age of nine saw a tree filled with angels. He was skilful at drawing and became apprentice to an engraver, who taught him how to illustrate books with pictures. He earned his living from engraving although he wrote poetry in his spare time.

At the age of 25, Blake married. Very soon his wife was helping him to print illustrated books of his poetry, which he did by etching his poems onto small copper plates. Pictures were then drawn in the margins and each page had to be printed and coloured one by one.

Blake's most popular book was published in 1794. This was *Songs of Innocence*, which included the 'happy songs ev'ry child may joy to hear.' Arguably Blake's most popular poem, 'The Tyger' was published five years later in *Songs of Experience*.

While Blake was alive, few people liked his work and some thought his paintings 'hideous'. A few people labelled him 'insane'. In his final years he was very poor although in 1818 he met a young artist who gave him money and helped to get his work noticed. Blake died in London in 1827.

Songs of Innocence and of Experience

This book contains some of Blake's finest poems, chosen from his original *Songs of* titles.

From: The Chimney-Sweeper

When my mother died I was very young,
And my father sold me while yet my tongue
Could scarcely cry "weep! weep! weep! weep!"
So your chimneys I sweep, and in soot I sleep.

There's little Tom Dacre, who cried when his head,
That curl'd like a lamb's back, was shav'd; so I said,
"Hush, Tom! Never mind it, for, when your head's bare,
You know that the soot cannot spoil your white hair."

(*William Blake – The Penguin Poets*, 1965).

Questions

What makes Blake's poems so special?
Blake believed that we see truths not just with our eyes but with our souls. His poetry comes not just from observations but from inner visions. His *Songs of Innocence* and *Songs of Experience* show the two contrasting sides to the soul – the lamb and the tiger. Blake used these contrasting animals to show that sometimes our souls are at peace (the lamb) and sometimes troubled, even angered (the tiger). Blake's wife once remarked that it was very hard to gain her husband's attention as he paid more attention to his visions than he did to her.

What inspired Blake?
Blake believed that visitors from the spirit world both guided and encouraged his imaginative work. He also wrote about events of his own age such as the American and French Revolutions – and about how industrialization in Britain was spoiling the countryside with factories.

Pie Corbett says:
'Blake used to see angels. That fascinates me. His poems seem so simple and yet they hold big truths. For instance, I love the idea of seeing the world in a grain of sand.'

Selected Bibliography

Books
Songs of Innocence and of Experience (Oxford Paperbacks); *The Complete Poems of William Blake* (Penguin); *Selected Poems of William Blake* (Penguin).

Videos
Famous Authors – William Blake, VHS tape (Academy Media).

Audio Books
Roger Lloyd Pack reads *William Blake's Selected Poems* (Rough Wind Productions).

weblinks
For more information about William Blake, go to
www.waylinks.co.uk/favclassicpoets

Alfred, Lord Tennyson (1809–92)

Draw near and fear not – this is I,
The Lady of Shalott.

Alfred, Lord Tennyson was born in Somersby, Lincolnshire. His father was a rector who lived with his wife and their twelve children at the rectory. Tennyson began writing at an early age and when he was 12 he composed a 6,000-line poem. At 18 he began to attend Cambridge University but was forced to leave in 1831 when his father died. For much of the 1830s he had very little money and not enough to allow him to marry.

His poems, however, gradually became better known and in 1850 he was appointed Poet Laureate. In the same year he finally married Emily Sellwood and they bought a home at Freshwater on the Isle of Wight, where they had three children. Even Queen Victoria's husband, Prince Albert visited the Tennysons in their new home, as did many visiting holidaymakers who tried to catch sight of the famous poet in his garden!

From: The Charge of the Light Brigade

I. *Half a league, half a league,*
    Half a league onward,
All in the valley of Death
    Rode the six hundred.
"Forward, the Light Brigade!
"Charge for the guns!" he said:
Into the valley of Death
    Rode the six hundred.

II. *"Forward, the Light Brigade!"*
Was there a man dismay'd?
Not tho' the soldier knew
    Someone had blunder'd:
Theirs not to make reply,
Theirs not to reason why,
Theirs but to do and die:
Into the valley of Death
    Rode the six hundred.

(*Maud & Other Poems*, 1855).

As Poet Laureate, Tennyson wrote many of his most famous poems including 'The Charge of the Light Brigade' and the 'Idylls of the King' – a series of poems about King Arthur and his knights. Tennyson died in October 1892, aged 83 years and is buried in Poets' Corner, Westminster Abbey.

Questions

What inspired Tennyson?

To begin with, writing poetry was an escape. Tennyson learned to retreat into his own private world to escape the trials and stresses of a father and brother who both suffered with mental illness. The grief that he felt at the death of his great friend Arthur Hallam in 1833 at the age of 22, lead to the writing of some of his best poetry including 'In Memoriam' – a tribute to his friend. 'The Charge of the Light Brigade' was written about a fatal mistake in the Crimean war against Russia. When British horse soldiers were ordered to charge the Russian guns it proved to be a suicidal attempt on the part of the British to overpower them.

What makes Tennyson's poems so special?

Tennyson's great friend Edward Fitzgerald wrote that the poet had, '... stocked the English language with lines which once knowing one can't forgo.' The poems are carefully composed with subtle rhythms. They also give a glimpse of what was valued and considered important in the age of Queen Victoria (1837–1901).

Judith Nicholls says:

'Tennyson can tell a tale and in *The Lady of Shalott* any unfamiliar language patterns are forgotten as he draws us along with the insistent rhythms and romantic mystery of the tale he tells.'

Selected Bibliography

Books

Selected Poems, edited by Aidan Day (Penguin); *Selected Poems* (Dover Publications); *Idylls of the King*, edited by J.M. Gray (Penguin); *The Lady of Shalott*, illustrated by Charles Keeping (Oxford University Press).

The Lady of Shalott
Alfred, Lord Tennyson
Illustrated by Charles Keeping

The Lady of Shalott

This is the romantic poem about the lovely and mysterious Lady of Shalott, on her silent isle, grieving with love for her knight, the brave Sir Lancelot.

weblinks

For more information about Alfred, Lord Tennyson, go to www.waylinks.co.uk/favclassicpoets

Robert Browning

(1812–1889)

Oh, to be in England
Now that April's there…

Robert Browning was born in London in 1812. His father was a bank clerk and very well-read. Robert didn't receive much formal schooling, but his father had over 6,000 books at home so he read widely. He learned many languages and began writing poems at quite an early age.

Browning's first book *Pauline* was published anonymously in 1833 and wasn't a success. However, between 1841 and 1846 four further books were published and these were to become some of his most famous works. In 1844 he read some poems by Elizabeth Barrett. He wrote to her for a few months before he met her. They decided to marry but Elizabeth's father did not approve. In 1846 they eloped and went to live in Florence in Italy where they continued to write poetry and had a son.

Sadly, Elizabeth did not enjoy good health and died in 1861. Robert Browning moved back to London. His fame spread during the 1860s until he had become almost as popular as Tennyson. His narrative poem 'The Pied Piper of Hamelin' was published in 1843 and written for the son of an actor friend. It was hailed as a children's classic.

From: The Pied Piper of Hamelin

I.

Hamelin Town's in Brunswick,
By famous Hanover city;
The river Weser, deep and wide,
Washes its wall on the southern side;
A pleasanter spot you never spied;
But, when begins my ditty,
Almost five hundred years ago,
To see the townsfolk suffer so
From vermin, was a pity.

II.

Rats!
They fought the dogs and killed the cats,
And bit the babies in the cradles,
And ate the cheeses out of the vats,
And licked the soup from the cooks'
own ladles,
Split open the kegs of salted sprats,
Made nests inside men's Sunday hats,
And even spoiled the women's chats
By drowning their speaking
With shrieking and squeaking
In fifty different sharps and flats.

(The Pied Piper of Hamelin,
Everyman Library).

David Orme says:
'I like Browning because so many of his poems end with a mystery. My favourite poem of all is called 'Child Roland to the Dark Tower Came'. I love the sense of terror and mystery.'

What makes Browning's poems so special? Browning is highly skilled at the dramatic monologue. This is where the writer creates a character and then speaks in the voice of that character about his feelings and his views of the world around him. Quite often this takes place at a point of crisis in the character's life.

What inspired Browning?

'The Pied Piper of Hamelin' was based on a folk tale about a piper who charmed rats out of a city with his pipe and then to a land inside a mountain. The legend may also be linked with the Children's Crusade of 1212 when thousands of children marched across Europe in a vain attempt to reach the Holy Land and help free it from the Saracens (Muslim Arabs).

Selected Bibliography

Books

Selected Poems, (Penguin); *The Poetical Works of Robert Browning* (Wordsworth Editions); *The Pied Piper of Hamelin*, (Orchard Books); *The Pied Piper of Hamelin* (Everyman Library).

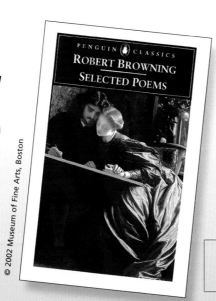

© 2002 Museum of Fine Arts, Boston

Robert Browning Selected Poems

This book contains many of the poet's most popular poems from his early years, as well as some of the less familiar poems written later in his life.

weblinks

For more information about Robert Browning, go to **www.waylinks.co.uk/favclassicpoets**

Edward Lear

'How pleasant to know Mr. Lear
    Who has written such volumes of stuff!
Some think him ill-tempered and queer,
    But a few think him pleasant enough.'

Edward Lear made money to live on by teaching drawing and selling his paintings. But then he began to concentrate on writing nonsense verse. More books were published in the 1870s and his most famous poem 'The Owl and the Pussycat' was written in December 1867 for the daughter of a friend.

Edward Lear was the 20th child in a family of 21 children and was born in London. He did not have a happy childhood but his eldest sister Ann taught him how to draw. She also helped him to cope with the epileptic fits that troubled him from the age of six.

He began a career as a draughtsman in Regent's Park Zoo when he was 19. In 1832 the Earl of Derby asked him to draw the rare birds that the Earl kept in his zoo at Knowsley Hall on Merseyside. He began to amuse the Earl's children with nonsense verses that he had written. In 1846 these were published as his first *Book of Nonsense*.

The Jumblies

They went to sea in a Sieve, they did,
    In a Sieve they went to sea:
In spite of all their friends could say,
On a winter's morn, on a stormy day,
    In a Sieve they went to sea!
And when the Sieve turned round and round,
And every one cried, 'You'll all be drowned!'
They called aloud, "Our Sieve ain't big,
But we don't care a button! We don't care a fig!
    In a Sieve we'll go to sea!"
        Far and few, far and few,
        Are the lands where the Jumblies live:
        Their heads are green, and their hands are blue,
        And they went to sea in a Sieve.

(The Complete Book of Nonsense, Faber, 1947).

Questions

What inspired Lear?

Although he travelled to paint landscapes, Lear's nonsense writing was inspired by the climate and the scenery of his visits. He was also inspired to write by the talk and behaviour of children. He enjoyed amusing them with his nonsense rhymes.

What is it that makes Lear's poems so special?

Lear had a natural gift for invention. He peopled his verses with odd characters – the Quangle Wangle, the Pobble Who Has No Toes, the Yonghy-Bonghy-Bo – and these characters have a timeless appeal. He loved to play with words and in one of his letters he wrote about 'Madame Pul-itz-neck-off.' Lear also wrote many limericks (short humorous verses) and made this form of verse popular:

There was a Young Lady of Russia,
Who screamed so that no one could hush her;
Her screams were extreme, no one heard such a scream
As was screamed by that lady of Russia.

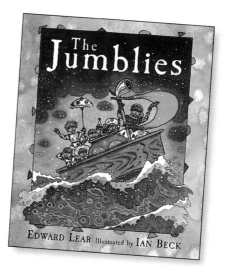

The Jumblies

This book brings to life the classic Lear rhyme about the Jumblies who go to sea in a sieve. With a pea-green sail and a tobacco-pipe mast, they travel to distant, mysterious lands and the hills of the Chankly Bore.

> **Roger Stevens says:**
> 'Edward Lear opened the door for future poets, such as myself, to write nonsense. He also made it quite acceptable for owls, hens, larks and wrens to nest in beards.'

Selected Bibliography

Books

The Complete Nonsense of Edward Lear, ed. Holbrook Jackson (Faber Children's Classics); *The Quangle Wangle's Hat*, illustrated by Helen Oxenbury (Mammoth); *The Owl and the Pussycat*, illustrated by Ian Beck (Picture Corgi); *The Jumblies*, illustrated by Ian Beck (Doubleday).

Audio Books

Edward Lear's Nonsense Stories and Poems (Caedmon Audio Cassette).

For more information about Edward Lear, go to
www.waylinks.co.uk/favclassicpoets

Christina Rossetti (1830–1894)

Regent's Park Zoo. She also enjoyed summer holidays at her grandfather's country cottage in Buckinghamshire. She was twice engaged to be married, but broke off the engagement each time.

Christina Rossetti's first book *Goblin Market* was published in 1862. The title poem is about two sisters who are tempted by goblins offering them fruit. *Sing-Song: A Nursery Rhyme Book* was published in 1872. In this book Christina Rossetti remembered her own childhood and perhaps escaped to a happier time, away from the ill-health from which she suffered in her later years. She died in December 1894 and is buried in Highgate Cemetery.

Remember me when I am gone away,
Gone far away into the silent land:
When you can no more hold me by the hand,
Nor I half turn to go yet turning stay.

Christina Rossetti was born in London in 1830. Her father had been a popular poet in Italy but had come to England as a refugee where he married an English governess. Christina was the youngest of four clever children and her brother was the famous painter, Dante Gabriel Rossetti. All the Rossetti children wrote poetry and received much encouragement from their parents.

The world of nature was of great interest to Christina and the family often visited

From: Spring

There is no time like Spring,
Like Spring that passes by;
There is no life like Spring life born to die, –
Piercing the sod,
Clothing the uncouth clod,
Hatched in the nest,
Fledged on the windy bough,
Strong on the wing:
There is no time like Spring that passes by,
Now newly born, and now
Hastening to die.

(The Complete Poems, Penguin).

Questions

What inspired Rossetti?

Christina was inspired by the natural world. In her early years she spent much time with her grandfather in the country which allowed her to be close to nature. She wrote about the changing seasons, the wind, lambs at play, a caterpillar. She seemed to have a special affection for small creatures such as lambs, puppies and birds. She also wrote a series of love poems and the much loved Christmas carol – 'In The Bleak Mid-Winter'. Her charitable works led her to write occasional poems with social themes such as poverty or inequality.

Christina Rossetti
The Complete Poems

This book features all the published poetry including sonnets, ballads, nursery rhymes and religious works of this popular poet.

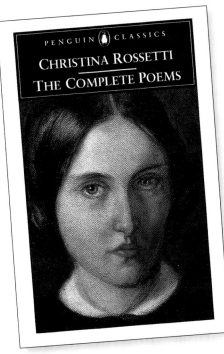

What is it that makes Rossetti's poems so special?

'Vitality', 'simplicity' and 'clearness' are three words used about her poems, but her poetry shouldn't be seen as too simple. Her poems often use spring as an image for childhood – when life is born again, or of how easy it is to let the seasons pass without really noticing them. She feels that children too can often fail to enjoy their younger years because they are impatient to see what lies ahead.

Naomi Lewis says:
'It [Rossetti's poetry] seems on the surface as clear as water, but the water is deep, with unsuspected tides.'

Selected Bibliography

Books

The Complete Poems, ed. Betty Flowers (Penguin); *Selected Poems of Christina Rossetti* (Wordsworth Editions); *Goblin Market and Other Poems* (Dover Publications); *Remember Me When I Am Gone* (Souvenir Press Ltd).

weblinks
For more information about Christina Rossetti, go to www.waylinks.co.uk/favclassicpoets

Rudyard Kipling (1865–1936)

"If you can keep your head when all about you
Are losing theirs and blaming it on you"

Rudyard Kipling was born in India. He and his sister Alice were sent back to England when he was six. The children stayed with foster parents and were dreadfully unhappy. Kipling was punished for reading books and began to read secretly by the light of a candle-end. Kipling was then sent to boarding school where he was encouraged to write. Later he returned to India where he worked as a journalist in Lahore. In his spare time he wrote many poems and stories. His first book of verse was published in 1886.

Returning to England in 1889 Kipling found that his stories had made him a popular figure. In 1892 he married and moved to America for four years where his two children, Josephine and Elsie were born. The family returned to England in 1896 and lived in Rottingdean in Sussex, where their son John was born. Sadly, Josephine died of pneumonia in 1899 and John was killed whilst fighting in the First World War (1914–18).

In 1902 he bought a house called Bateman's in Sussex where he lived for the rest of his life. It was at this house that his best known poem, 'If . . .' was written. Kipling declined the offer of Poet Laureateship but was the first English writer to be awarded the Nobel Prize for Literature in 1907. Kipling died in 1936 and was buried in Poets' Corner in Westminster Abbey.

From: A Smuggler's Song

If you wake at midnight, and hear a horse's feet,
Don't go drawing back the blind, or looking in the street,
Them that asks no questions isn't told a lie
Watch the wall, my darling, while the Gentlemen go by!
    Five and twenty ponies
    Trotting through the dark –
    Brandy for the Parson,
    'Baccy for the Clerk;
    Laces for a Lady, letters for a Spy,
Watch the wall, my darling, while the Gentlemen go by!

Running round the woodlump if you chance to find
Little barrels, roped and tarred, all full of brandy-wine,
Don't you shout to come and look, nor use 'em for your play.
Put the brushwood back again – and they'll be gone next day!

(The Works of Rudyard Kipling, Wordsworth Editions).

What inspired Kipling?

Kipling wrote a lot about India although he only spent six and a half years there. He wrote rhymed verse, some of it in the slang used by British soldiers in India, and he invented fictional characters such as Gunga Din and Danny Deever.

What is it that makes Kipling's poems so special?

Kipling's poems reach out to lots of people. They are not difficult to understand and can be enjoyed by anyone, not just poetry specialists. His poetry is often labelled patriotic – displaying a love of his country and its empire.

Peter Dixon says:
'I'm not really into flags and armies or Limpopo Rivers, but I love thundering good poems that tell a story. That's what Rudyard Kipling did best.'

Selected Bibliography

Books
Kipling: Poems (Everyman); *The Works of Rudyard Kipling* (Wordsworth Editions); *Gunga Din and Other Favourite Poems* (Dover Publications).

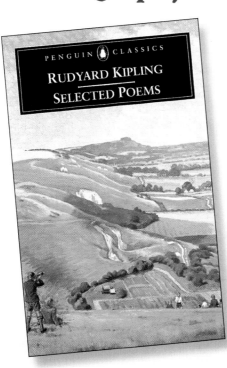

PENGUIN CLASSICS
RUDYARD KIPLING
SELECTED POEMS

Rudyard Kipling Selected Poems
This book has a selection of Kipling's poetry, and shows the development of his work through the years.

Audio Books
The Poetry of Rudyard Kipling (HarperCollins).

weblinks
For more information about Rudyard Kipling, go to www.waylinks.co.uk/favclassicpoets

Hilaire Belloc

Matilda told such Dreadful Lies,
It made one Gasp and Stretch one's Eyes . . .

Hilaire Belloc was born in the French town of La Celle St. Cloud near Paris in July 1870, the son of a French father and an English mother. The family left France in 1872 during the Franco-Prussian war and settled in Sussex. Belloc attended the Oratory School in Birmingham and later, Balliol College, Oxford. In between the two he met his future wife who was visiting Europe from America, hitchhiked to California to propose to her and then spent a year in the French army.

The Yak

As a friend to the children
Commend me the Yak.
You will find it exactly the thing:
It will carry and fetch, you can ride on its back,
Or lead it about with a string.
The Tartar who dwells on the plains of Thibet
(A desolate region of snow)
Has for centuries made it a nursery pet,
And surely the Tartar should know!
Then tell your papa where the Yak can be got,
And if he is awfully rich
He will buy you the creature –
or else
    he will not.
(I cannot be positive which.)

(The Bad Child's Book of Beasts, 1896).

Belloc married his fiancée in 1896, the same year as the publication of his book, *The Bad Child's Book of Beasts*. This collection of nonsensical verse for children met with immediate success. *More Beasts for Worst Children* followed in 1897, *A Moral Alphabet* in 1899 and *Cautionary Tales* in 1907. From 1896 until 1942 he wrote 156 books including biographies, travel books, novels and both serious and comic verse. In his personal life, Belloc faced tragedy on a number of occasions. His wife died in 1914, and his sons died in the World Wars. Belloc continued to write and to lecture about his writing until 1942 when he had a suffered a stroke. He died in Sussex in 1953, a few days after losing his balance and falling into his study's fireplace.

What inspired Belloc?

His love for Sussex inspired some of his verse along with the journeys that he made and the places he visited. He had a macabre sense of humour which was evident from *Cautionary Tales*. It included such titles as 'Jim Who Ran Away From His Nurse and Was Eaten by a Lion' and 'Algernon, Who Played with a Loaded Gun, and, on Missing his Sister, was Reprimanded by his Father' and the popular 'Matilda Who Told Lies, and was Burned to Death.'

Cautionary Verses
When this book was published in 1907, as *Cautionary Tales*, it proved particularly popular with children.

What makes Belloc's verse so special?

Belloc's books of verse for children were spoken of as being some of the funniest poems for children since those of Edward Lear. Belloc worked hard at the verses until the rhythm was exact and there was not a syllable out of place. Belloc's poems are still popular today with both children and adults. Children enjoy Belloc's *Cautionary Verses* because of their gruesome elements, in the same way as they enjoy Raold Dahl's *Revolting Rhymes*. Adults often read them too, finding them easy to learn by heart.

Selected Bibliography

Books
Cautionary Verses (Templegate Publishers); *Complete Verse* (Pimlico).

weblinks
For more information about Hilaire Belloc, go to www.waylinks.co.uk/favclassicpoets

Walter de la Mare

*"Is there anybody there?" said the traveller
knocking on the moonlit door.*

Walter de la Mare was born in Charlton, a village in Kent, in 1873. He attended St Paul's Choir School in London and then left at the age of sixteen to start work with an oil company. It wasn't a very interesting job but he stayed there for 18 years. He had begun writing poems and stories while still at school and when he started work he continued in his lunch hours and in the evenings. He would often write on crumpled up pieces of graph paper that he rescued from the wastepaper basket.

Winter

*Clouded with snow
The cold winds blow,
And shrill on leafless bough
The robin with its burning breast
Alone sings now.
The rayless sun,
Day's journey done,
Sheds its last ebbing light
On fields in leagues of beauty spread
Unearthly white.
Thick draws the dark,
And spark by spark,
The frost-fires kindle, and soon
Over that sea of frozen foam
Floats the white moon.*

(The Listeners & Other Poems, 1912).

In 1895 de la Mare sold his first story. The following years brought a few more successes but also many rejections. In August 1899 he married, and had a son and daughter. He was now writing many poems for children, and each night he would read them to his own children to test their reactions.

In 1908 he was awarded a government pension for his writing. This meant that he could stop work at the oil company. A collection of children's poems, *Peacock Pie*, was published in 1913. His best known poem is probably 'The Listeners.'

Questions

Judith Nicholls says:
'For anyone who loves Charles Causley's poems (as I do) he [Walter de la Mare] is well worth delving into. Some of his poems are timeless: and like Charles Causley, he knows how to make words sing and echo with meaning far beyond their apparent simplicity.'

What is it that makes de la Mare's poems so special?

Writer Eleanor Graham says: 'One of the tremendously exciting things about Walter de la Mare's poetry is the way it lights up the reader's own experiences by the clearness and strength of the poet's vision.' De la Mare had the ability to put himself into the mind of a child and to describe things in the way that children see them. He hoped that he might look at the world and keep even the smallest things in his memory forever.

What inspired de la Mare?

He drew much of his inspiration from his love of the countryside around his home. He also observed children and their activities, finding links with memories from his own childhood. He was also very imaginative, liking to explore the world between the real and the unreal.

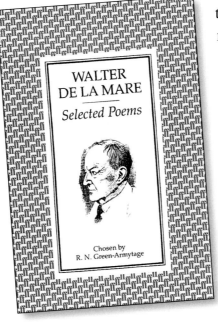

Walter de la Mare Selected Poems

This book contains many of Walter de la Mare's best known poems. In his writing he celebrates the beauty of nature, and reflects on the meaning of life. His vivid imagination entertains readers of all ages.

Selected Bibliography

Books

Peacock Pie (Faber Children's Books); *Selected Poems of Walter de la Mare* (Faber & Faber); *Collected Rhymes and Verses* (Faber & Faber).

Audio Books

Peacock Pie is available from the Audio Book & Music Company.

Robert Frost

(1874–1963)

Two roads diverged in a wood, and I –
I took the one less travelled by,
And that made all the difference.

Robert Frost was one of America's greatest poets. He was born in San Francisco in 1874. He was unable to go to school because he suffered with nervous stomach pains whenever he tried to attend. His mother, who was a teacher, taught him at home. Frost's father died when he was 11 and the family moved across country to New England. There he attended a high school where he achieved excellent results.

Whilst at high school Frost began writing poems. After he finished school he went to college but left before completing his degree. His poetry met with little success and he tried several jobs before becoming a poultry farmer in New Hampshire.

In 1895 he married a former classmate and they had six children, although two of them died at a very young age. In 1912 Frost moved his family to England. He found a London publisher prepared to publish a book of his poems. *A Boy's Will* came out in 1913 and a second book a year later.

Stopping by Woods on a Snowy Evening

Whose woods these are I think I know.
His house is in the village though;
He will not see me stopping here
To watch his woods fill up with snow.

My little horse must think it queer
To stop without a farmhouse near
Between the woods and frozen lake
The darkest evening of the year.

He gives his harness bells a shake
To ask if there is some mistake.
The only other sound's the sweep
Of easy wind and downy flake.

The woods are lovely, dark and deep.
But I have promises to keep,
And miles to go before I sleep,
And miles to go before I sleep.

(*You Come Too*, The Bodley Head, 1964).

In 1915 the Frost family went back to America. By the 1920s Frost was the most popular poet in the USA and spent the rest of his life writing poetry and managing his farm.

Questions

What inspired Frost?

Frost's wife Elinor Miriam White was a major inspiration in his poetry until her death in 1938. Frost was also greatly inspired in his writing by the people and landscape of New England. He became known as 'the essential voice and spirit' of the place.

What makes Frost's poems so special?

Frost was much more than just a poet writing about life in the countryside. Frost once stated his ambition as, to write 'a few poems it will be hard to get rid of.' In this he certainly succeeded as many of his poems are both powerful and memorable. His rural and rhythmical verse won many literary prizes in America.

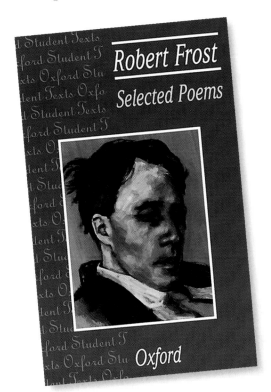

Wes Magee says:

'I greatly admire Robert Frost's ability to paint vivid word pictures of landscapes. His poem 'Stopping by Woods on a Snowy Evening' is a visual masterpiece. The sense of winter and snow makes you shiver with cold . . .'

Robert Frost
Selected Poems

This book includes 40 poems from nine collections, providing a good introduction to Frost's poetry.

Selected Bibliography

Books

A Child's Year of Stories and Poems (Viking Children's Books); *Selected Poems* (Oxford University Press); *Stopping by Woods on a Snowy Evening*, illustrated by Susan Jeffers (Dutton Books); *You Come Too: Favourite Poems for Younger Readers* (Owl Publishing Company).

Audio Books

Robert Frost Poetry Collection (Caedmon Audio Cassette); *The Poetry of Robert Frost* (New Millennium Audio).

weblinks

For more information about Robert Frost, go to
www.waylinks.co.uk/favclassicpoets

Alfred Noyes

Everyone grumbled. The sky was grey.
We had nothing to do and nothing to say.
We were nearing the end of a dismal day.
And there seemed to be nothing beyond,
   Then
      Daddy fell into the pond!

Alfred Noyes was born in Wolverhampton in 1880. He was the eldest of three sons and a daughter, and he spent his boyhood in Aberystwyth, Wales, where his father was a teacher. At 18 he went to Oxford University where he was very good at rowing but failed to complete his degree. Instead he was visiting a publisher who wanted to publish his first book of poems, which appeared in 1902. Two years later he wrote his most famous poem, 'The Highwayman', inspired by a blustery night on Bagshot Heath, Surrey, where Noyes was living in a tiny cottage.

Noyes' poems were as popular in the USA as they were in Britain. He lived in America on two occasions. Once between 1914 and 1923 when he was a professor of modern English Literature at Princetown University, and again during World War II (1939–45). From 1932 to 1958 Alfred Noyes mainly lived on the Isle of Wight where his hobbies were swimming, rowing and golf. In his later years his sight failed and he began to dictate his work rather than write it down.

From: The Highwayman

The wind was a torrent of darkness upon the gusty trees,
The moon was a ghostly galleon tossed upon cloudy seas,
The road was a ribbon of moonlight over the purple moor,
And the highwayman came riding –
   Riding – riding –
The highwayman came riding, up to the old inn-door.
He'd a French cocked hat on his forehead, a bunch of lace at his chin;
A coat of the claret velvet, and breeches of brown doeskin.
They fitted with never a wrinkle; his boots were up to the thigh!
And he rode with a jewelled twinkle –
His pistol butts a-twinkle,
His rapier hilt a-twinkle, under the jewelled sky.

(Selected Poems, J. Murray, 1950).

Questions

What inspired Noyes?

Initially the Welsh coastline and the mountains around his childhood home in Aberystwyth inspired Noyes. When he became a Roman Catholic in 1927 his religious views began to influence his work.

The Highwayman

This is the story of the Highwayman's doomed love for Bess, the landlord's black-eyed daughter.

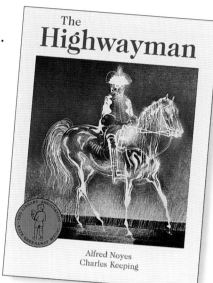

The
Highwayman

Alfred Noyes
Charles Keeping

What makes Noyes' poems so special?

'The Highwayman' is a favourite poem for many people. It is a narrative poem, both dramatic and atmospheric. Many readers discover this poem while young and get caught up in the enjoyment of the adventure. In his humorous poem 'Daddy Fell into the Pond', we see a different side of Noyes. One writer said of Noyes, '. . . he was gifted alike with the power of seeing and the power of imparting beauty to others.'

Pie Corbett says:

'I've read 'The Highwayman' a thousand times. It's a great poem – full of romance, danger, adventure and death. It would make a great film. The use of imagery makes the poem very visual.'

Selected Bibliography

Books

The Highwayman, illustrated by Charles Keeping (OUP). This poem and 'Daddy Fell into the Pond' can also be found in *I Like this Poem*, ed. Kay Webb (Puffin).

weblinks

For more information about Alfred Noyes, go to
www.waylinks.co.uk/favclassicpoets

Eleanor Farjeon

(1881–1965)

Once Upon a Time,
Once Upon a Time!
Everything that happened, happened
Once Upon a Time!

Eleanor Farjeon was born in London. Her father was a writer and he passed on to Eleanor his love of storytelling. She grew up in a house surrounded by books – the 'little bookroom' was an attic space piled with books. Her father encouraged his daughter and her three brothers to compose their own stories and poems from an early age. Eleanor Farjeon once wrote, 'It would have been more natural to live without clothes than without books.'

The Farjeon children were taught at home by a governess. Eleanor wore glasses from the age of eight and as a child was described as being small, shy and quiet. At 18 she wrote the lyrics for an operetta, performed in London, with music composed by her brother. Her first successful book was *Nursery Rhymes of London Town*, published in 1916. In this book she gave witty explanations for the origins of many London place names such as King's Cross and Blackfriars.

Eleanor was friends with many other poets such as Walter de la Mare, Edward Thomas and Robert Frost. Her poem 'Morning Has Broken' has become a popular hymn that is often sung in school assemblies. Many of her books are strikingly illustrated by Edward Ardizzone. 'All I feel about childhood is in them', she once wrote about his illustrations.

School-Bell

Nine-o'Clock Bell!
Nine-o'Clock Bell!
All the small children and big ones as well,
Pulling their stockings up, snatching their hats,
Checking and grumbling and giving back-chats,
Laughing and quarrelling, dropping their things,
These at a snail's pace and those upon wings,
Lagging behind a bit, running ahead,
Waiting at corners for lights to turn red,
Some of them scurrying,
Others not worrying,
Carelessly trudging or anxiously hurrying,
All through the streets they are coming pell-mell
At the Nine-o'Clock
Nine-o'Clock
Nine-o'Clock
Bell!

(Blackbird has Spoken – Selected Poems for Children, Macmillan, 1999).

What inspired Farjeon?

An early interest in fairy tales seems to have helped develop Eleanor's imaginative powers. The range and variety of her imagination was immense. She enjoyed making links between fantasy and reality and this can be seen in her *Nursery Rhymes of London Town*. She would take a name, such as King's Cross, and imagine it was a cross king, throwing his sceptre into the Thames. Seeing the world through children's eyes was one of her strengths.

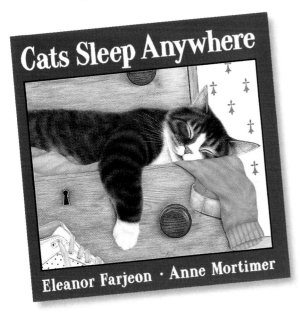

What makes Farjeon's poems so special?

Her poems are witty, often humorous, sometimes nonsensical. Many express her wonder at the world and her enchantment with the small details of everyday events. She is also skilful at remembering the emotions of childhood and writing of them in her poetry.

Cats Sleep Anywhere

A beautifully illustrated poem about cats written with keen observation and gentle humour.

Selected Bibliography

Books

Blackbird Has Spoken – Selected Poems for Children, chosen by Anne Harvey (Macmillan Children's Books); *Cats Sleep Anywhere*, illustrated by Anne Mortimer (Frances Lincoln); *Elsie Piddock Skips in Her Sleep*, illustrated by Charlotte Voake (Walker Books).

Songs

The poem 'Morning has Broken' was set to music by Cat Stevens in the early 1970s.

weblinks
For more information about Eleanor Farjeon, go to
www.waylinks.co.uk/favclassicpoets

Hush, hush, whisper who dares,
Christopher Robin is saying his prayers.

(1914–18) he also wrote a play for children, published in 1917. On a holiday in Wales he shut himself away in a summerhouse for eleven days and wrote a large amount of verse for children. These were then published along with others in *Punch* magazine and then in a book *When We Were Very Young* in 1924, which was very successful. A second book *Now We Are Six* was published in 1927, a year after the first of his *Winnie-the-Pooh* story books.

The More it Snows

The more it
SNOWS-tiddely-pom,
The more it
GOES-tiddely-pom,
The more it
GOES-tiddely-pom.
On
Snowing.

And nobody
KNOWS-tiddely-pom.
How cold my
TOES-tiddely-pom,
How cold my
TOES-tiddely-pom,
Are
Growing.

(The House at Pooh Corner,
1928).

Alan Alexander Milne was born in London. His father was a schoolmaster, and for a brief time one of his fellow teachers was H.G. Wells, the science fiction writer. He was the third of three sons. Alan and his brother Ken spent a lot of time together. They both won scholarships to Westminster school and began composing verse. Alan went on to Cambridge University where he continued writing light verse and humorous prose and his first efforts were published in the magazine *Punch*. He was later asked to become assistant editor of the magazine.

A.A. Milne married Daphne in 1913 and had one son, Christopher Robin. While he was on active service during World World War I

Questions

What inspired A.A. Milne?

Milne once wrote, 'There are three ways in which a writer knows about people: by remembering, by noticing and by imagining.' In his writing Milne often remembered his childhood, particularly the long walks and adventures that he shared with his brother Ken as they were growing up.

He noticed his wife Daphne playing with their son, Christopher Robin and was inspired by the stories of toy animals that she told to him. And he imagined a world of fairy folk who featured in some of his poems.

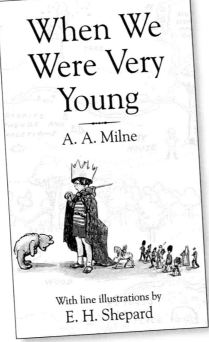

When We Were Very Young

A. A. Milne

With line illustrations by
E. H. Shepard

When We Were Very Young

This first poetry book can be enjoyed at any age, as the verse appeals to the child within all of us. The timeless quality of the poems make them enjoyable for different generations.

What makes A.A. Milne's poems so special?

A.A. Milne's verse is admired for being technically good even though it is only light verse intended for children in the nursery. Reading his poems aloud enables us to see just how the rhymes work together in helping to make the poems memorable.

David Harmer says:
'A.A. Milne is the poet who taught me how to make the best use of rhyme.'

Selected Bibliography

Books

When We Were Very Young, illustrated by Ernest H. Shepard (Methuen Young Books); *Now We Are Six*, illustrated by Ernest H. Shepard (Methuen Young Books); *The Complete Winnie-the-Pooh*, illustrated by Ernest H. Shepard (Hamlyn Young Books).

Audio Books

When We Were Very Young and *Now We Are Six* (Caedmon Audio Cassette).

weblinks
For more information about A.A. Milne, go to
www.waylinks.co.uk/favclassicpoets

Langston Hughes

(1902–1967)

Just because I loves you –
That's de reason why
Ma soul is full of color
Like de wings of a butterfly.

Langston Hughes was born in Missouri, USA. His childhood was spent moving around the American Mid-West with his mother who was constantly looking for work. He once wrote that he slept in 'ten thousand beds' while growing up. Hughes had his first poems published while he was at school in Cleveland, Ohio where he also experienced racial taunts for the first time. When he left school he worked as a ranch-hand in Mexico and then began to travel the world earning a living in whatever place he found himself.

Throughout his travels he continued to write, sending poetry back home where some of it was published. Hughes had his first volume of poetry published in 1926, followed by a second a year later.

From 1925–29 he attended the nation's first African-American college, Lincoln University, in Pennsylvania. From then on, he lived by his writing, becoming one of the first African-Americans to achieve this. He was also the first African-American to write civil rights protest poetry. During his lifetime he produced over fifty books including novels, plays and poetry.

Mother to Son

Well, son, I'll tell you:
Life for me ain't been no crystal stair.
It's had tacks in it,
And splinters,
And boards torn up,
And places with no carpet on the floor –
Bare.
But all the time
I'se been a-climbin' on,
And reachin' landin's,
And turnin' corners,
And sometimes goin' in the dark
Where there ain't been no light.
So, boy, don't you turn back;
Don't you set down on the steps
'Cause you find it's kinder hard.
Don't you fall now –
For I'se still goin', honey,
I'se still climbin',
And life for me ain't been no crystal stair.

(Selected Poems, Serpent's Tail, 1999).

What inspired Hughes?

Hughes's writing was inspired and influenced by his life in Harlem, a predominantly African American district of New York City. He became known as 'The Poet Laureate of Harlem' spending a lot of time in the blues and jazz clubs of Harlem, and tried to write poems that were like the songs he heard. [These songs] '... had the pulse beat of the people who keep on going.'

Pie Corbett says:
'Langston Hughes' poems have a gentle warmth. They are often quite small but chime a memorable note that echoes long after reading.'

What makes Hughes's poetry so special?

His poetry gives an insight into the ordinary lives of black people in America from the 1920s onwards. Hughes was a poet who championed equality, condemned racism and stood up for black culture. The poems are rhythmical and in Hughes' words are written, '... to be read aloud, crooned, shouted and sung.' Many poems were set to music using the rhythms of jazz and blues.

The Dream Keeper and other poems

A lovely selection of the best of this poet's work. Hughes wrote about dreams and freedom in an optimistic way. In his poetry he helped black Americans to feel happy and proud and to stand up for themselves.

Selected Bibliography

Books
Selected Poems (Serpent's Tail);
The Dream Keeper and Other Poems (Alfred A. Knopf).

Audio Books
Langston Hughes Reads His Poetry (HarperAudio).

weblinks
For more information about Langston Hughes, go to www.waylinks.co.uk/favclassicpoets

Other favourite classic poets

There are so many excellent classic poets for you to get to know. Here are a few more introductions. Have a look for their poems in your public library or bookshop.

Robert Burns (1759–96)

Robert Burns is Scotland's best-loved poet. He was born on a small farm in Ayrshire, one of seven children, and began writing poetry at school. He carried on writing in his spare time while he worked on a farm. His first book *Poems, Chiefly in the Scottish Dialect*, published in 1786, was a big success. Burns wasn't able to live by his writing alone and in 1791 he took a job as a tax collector, making sure that tax was paid on goods coming into his part of Scotland. He moved to Dumfries with his family and when he wasn't working spent time putting new words to traditional Scottish tunes. His most celebrated poem, 'Tam o' Shanter' was published in 1791. Unfortunately Burns suffered from a weak heart and he died at the young age of 37. Today, wherever Scots are in the world, his genius is celebrated on his birthday, 25 January, known as Burns Night.

William Wordsworth (1770–1850)

William Wordsworth was born in Cockermouth, Cumberland. The River Derwent flowed past the back of the house and the young Wordsworth liked to play and enjoy adventures along its banks. Wordsworth's mother died when he was eight and his father when he was 13.

He went to live in lodgings in Hawkshead where he attended grammar school and where he was encouraged to write poetry. In 1795 he received some money which enabled him to concentrate on his writing. He lived with his sister Dorothy in Dorset where they met the poet Samuel Taylor Coleridge. The two poets worked on a book together and *Lyrical Ballads* was published in 1798. Wordsworth and Dorothy then moved to the Lake District, an area that inspired much of his writing. In 1802 he married his childhood friend, Mary Hutchinson. Wordsworth was Poet Laureate from 1843 until his death in 1850. His best known poems include 'Daffodils', 'Tintern Abbey' and 'Composed Upon Westminster Bridge'.

Henry Wadsworth Longfellow (1807–82)

Henry Wadsworth Longfellow was born and grew up in New England, USA. He started writing poetry in a serious way when he went to college and although his father wanted him to be a lawyer, he was determined that he would be a writer. He studied languages in Europe and returned to become a professor at his old college. He married twice, his first wife having died after a miscarriage. He wrote a lot about the sea, inspired by his childhood on the coast in Portland and his poems 'The Wreck of the Hesperus' and 'The Tide Rises, the Tide Falls' are examples of his love of the sea. He enjoyed writing long narrative poems, which included 'The Song of Hiawatha', which describes the life of an Indian brave.

Emily Dickinson (1830–86)

Emily Dickinson was born in Massachusetts, USA. She lived nearly all her life in the town of Amherst apart from visits to Washington and Philadelphia in her twenties. She wrote over 1,700 poems, which she kept in small handmade notebooks, and although she showed them to her friends, and to an editor, only seven poems were published while she was alive. Her life would appear to have been rather unhappy. Her health was delicate and for the final twenty-five years of her life she hardly seems to have left her house. She was terrified of thunderstorms but they were the inspiration for some of her finest poems. It was only after her death that she was recognized as one of America's most talented poets.

Because I could not stop for Death
He kindly stopped for me.
The carriage held but just ourselves
And immortality.

Robert Louis Stevenson (1850–94)

Robert Louis Stevenson was born in Edinburgh. His father was a lighthouse engineer and his mother a minister's daughter. He suffered with poor health for much of his childhood and it is now thought that he had tuberculosis. When he was 17 he went to Edinburgh University to study engineering but by the time he left he had decided that he wanted to be a writer. He wrote mainly adventure stories and travel books and in 1880 he married an American divorcee, Fanny Osbourne. They moved to France to try to find a warmer climate and it was there that he wrote most of the poems that were included in *A Child's Garden of Verses*. This is widely regarded as one of the finest books of poetry ever written for children. For the last five years of his life he lived on the island of Samoa in the South Pacific where the climate suited him.

T.S. Eliot (1888–1965)

Thomas Stearns Eliot was born in Missouri, USA. and lived in the city of St. Louis until he was 18. He then studied at Harvard University and at the Sorbonne in Paris. In 1914 he moved to England and worked as a teacher and then a bank clerk. His poem 'The Waste Land' was considered by many to be the most important poem published in the twentieth century. T.S. Eliot's friend, the poet Ezra Pound, nicknamed him 'Old Possum' and in 1939 Eliot published a book that was different from anything he had written before. He called it *Old Possum's Book of Practical Cats*. These poems were later the inspiration for the musical 'Cats'; poems set to music by Andrew Lloyd Webber.

Acknowledgements

The Publishers would like to thank the following publishers and illustrators who allowed us to use material in this book.

Poems

'The Jumblies' by Edward Lear from *The Complete Book of Nonsense*, Faber, 1947.

'If' and 'The Smuggler's Song' by Rudyard Kipling by permission of A.P. Watt Ltd on behalf of The National Trust for Places of Historical Interest or Natural Beauty.

'The Yak' and 'Matilda' by Hilaire Belloc reprinted by permission of PFD on behalf of The Estate of Hilaire Belloc, copyright © as printed in the original volume.

'The Traveller' and 'Winter' by Walter de la Mare by permission of The Literary Trustees of Walter de la Mare and the Society of Authors as their representative.

'The Road Not Taken' and 'Stopping by Woods on a Snowy Evening' from *The Poetry of Robert Frost*, edited by Edward Connery Lathem, the Estate of Robert Frost and Jonathan Cape as publisher. Used by permission of The Random House Group Limited.

'Daddy Fell into the Pond' and 'The Highwayman' by permission of The Literary Trustees of Alfred Noyes and the Society of Authors as their representative.

'School-Bell' by Eleanor Farjeon by permission of David Higham Associates.

'Just because I loves you' and 'Mother to Son' by Langston Hughes. Used by permission of The Random House Group Limited and Alfred A. Knopf.

Jackets and illustrations

Front cover from *Songs of Innocence and of Experience* by William Blake by permission of Oxford University Press.

Front cover and illustration from *The Lady of Shalott* by Alfred Lord Tennyson, illustrated by Charles Keeping, by permission of Oxford University Press.

Front cover from *Selected Poems of Robert Browning* reproduced by permission of Penguin, copyright © 2002 Museum of Fine Arts. Illustration from *The Pied Piper of Hamelin*, illustrated by Andre Amstutz. First published in the UK by Orchard Books in 1993, a division of The Watts Publishing Group Limited, 96 Leonard Street, London, EC2A 4XD. Also appears on the *title page*.

Front cover from *The Jumblies* by Edward Lear illustrated by Ian Beck, reprinted by permission of The Random House Group Limited. Also reproduced on the *cover*.

Front cover from *The Complete Poems of Christina Rossetti* reproduced by permission of Penguin.

Front cover from *Selected Poems of Rudyard Kipling* reproduced by permission of Penguin.

Front cover from *Cautionary Verses* by Hilaire Belloc, published by Red Fox. Reprinted by permission of The Random House Group Limited.

Front cover from *Selected Poems of Walter de la Mare* by permission of Faber & Faber Ltd.

Front cover from *Selected Poems of Robert Frost* published in 1998, by permission of Oxford University Press. Also reproduced on the *cover*.

Front cover from *The Highwayman* by Alfred Noyes, illustrated by Charles Keeping, by permission of Oxford University Press.

Front cover from *Cats Sleep Anywhere* by Eleanor Farjeon illustrated by Anne Mortimer published by Frances Lincoln Ltd, copyright © Frances Lincoln Ltd, 1996. Text copyright © Gervase Farjeon 1957, illustrations copyright © Anne Mortimer 1996. Reproduced by permission of Frances Lincoln Ltd., 4 Torriano Mews, Torriano Avenue, London NW5 2RZ. www.franceslincoln.com.

Front cover from *When We Were Very Young* copyright © E.H. Shepard and Egmont Books Ltd., reproduced by permission of Curtis Brown Ltd., London. Also reproduced on the *cover*.

Front cover from *The Dream Keeper and other Poems* by Langston Hughes, illustrated by J. Brian Pinkney. Illustrations copyright © 1994 by J. Brian Pinkney. Used by permission of Alfred A. Knopf, an imprint of Random House Children's Books, a division of Random House, Inc.

Photographs

The Publishers would like to thank the following for providing photographs: The Eleanor Farjeon Estate (Eleanor Farjeon outside her Sussex cottage in 1917) 25 & *cover*; Hodder Wayland Picture Library 5 & *cover*, Hulton-Getty Picture Collection Ltd 8, 10, 12, 15, 16, 18, 20, 23, 26, 28 & *cover*; Mary Evans Picture Library 6.

All possible care has been taken to trace the ownership of each poem included in this selection and to obtain copyright permission for its use. If there are any omissions or if any errors have occurred, they will be corrected in subsequent editions, on notification to the Publishers.